ADVENTURES WITH BYRON

*Love Poems and Entertaining Stories of Life
With an Enchanting Feline Companion*

Rosemary Augustine

Adventures with Byron
Love Poems and Entertaining Stories
  Of Life With an Enchanting Feline Companion
By Rosemary Augustine

Copyright © 2015 Rosemary Augustine

All Rights Reserved. No part of this book may be reproduced or transmitted in any form or by any means, electronic or mechanical, including photocopying, faxing, recording, emailing, posting on social media or by any information storage and retrieval system, or used for any other purpose without written permission from the author.

Published by:
Blue Spruce Publishing Company
2175 Golf Isle Drive, Suite 1024
Melbourne, FL 32935
610.647.8863
info@BlueSprucePublishing.com

Cover Photo: "Byron" by Rosemary Augustine
Photos of Bryon by Rosemary Augustine
Photos of Byron and Rosemary By Patricia Giannascoli
Photos of Bryon and Maxx by Rosemary Augustine
Photo of The Cat Spa - provided by CatSpaKennel.com
Photo of the Moon - Painting by Rosemary Augustine
Interior Cat Graphics: www.OpenClipArt.org
Keyboard Graphic: ^..^ by Rosemary Augustine
= ° =

ISBN-13: 978-1-943581-01-6
ISBN-10: 1-943581-01-0

DEDICATION

This book is dedicated to the memory of Byron – my companion for 18+ years, who often had human qualities and shared memorable moments either created by him or others. In addition, this book is also dedicated to anyone who had a "Byron" and shared similar experiences. Those individuals know a love deeper than imaginable.

^..^
=º=

INTRODUCTION

It was February 1985 when a black and white tuxedo kitty was born. He had a black nose instead of the traditional kitty pink. His first six months are unknown, but likely a weaning away from his mother and adopted by a family that wanted a cute pet. When fall came along with the usual back to school busyness, an influx of kitties started to show up at the local pound, including the future Byron.

This particular kitty was found wandering south of Sheridan and Hampden Blvds., in Southwest Denver in early November of that same year. Others say he wandered the streets of southwest Denver for months. However, Byron seemed too domesticated to be a wild one in the early months of his life.

It was a Sunday afternoon in November that his fate would change. I walked into the animal shelter looking for a special kitty to share my new condo. There was row after row of cats that ignored me.

As I walked the aisles, I fancied many a feline, but none noticed me. They would turn their back when I would peer through the glass and make funny faces. I figured if they didn't like my silliness now, they certainly wouldn't enjoy my adventurous lifestyle. I kept walking the aisles.

I had just about given up as I neared the last few cages of cats, until I set eyes on a special black and white kitty with the black button nose. His attention-getting tactics won my heart, and his purr reverberated off the concrete walls. His markings gave him a smile... a broad smile, almost a grin. I thought he looked like a poet... namely, Lord Byron!

I learned he would have been put to sleep the next morning had I not selected him. For the next 18+ years we shared laughs, secrets, love, and joys, two cross country trips, including a winter in Florida and a relocation to New Jersey and Pennsylvania.

Byron had many friends, including Fluffy, Drac, and his adopted brother Maxx. He enjoyed stalking birds, squirrels, and rabbits. He loved riding in the car and lying in the sun. Cuts, bruises, and illnesses from crystals in his urine, to fang bites and cornea scratches didn't deter him.

His best moment was grinning at me with that fang smile he was so famous for, while a piece of chicken dangled from his mouth like a dead rat.

Kitty aerobics was his specialty at 4:15 a.m. when he'd jump on the bed, getting a running start from the stairs in the hallway and carefully land on my stomach. He would then bounce off and onto the windowsill.

Byron was always the center of attention, certainly an extravert at the center of any party, greeting all the guests with his "please pet me" lounge act. His first Christmas, he was so excited to have a real tree, he climbed it while it sat in the living room.

Byron was a good judge of character and didn't hesitate to hiss at those he met and didn't like – man or beast. Few were afraid of him, most were in awe of him.

His markings and stature suited his namesake. And his presence when he entered a room made people stop and stare. He graced the floor like an oriental carpet. He was the grandest of the grand...Lord Byron, King Kat of the Augustine household. He made all the rules for others to live by while smiling at you with that toothy fang grin. His classic pose was on his back waiting for a belly rub. And, his favorite spot in the house? Anywhere there was sunshine. He was special yet enchanting at the same time.

While Byron was alive, I often joked about him modeling for magazines or cat food or submitting his picture for a cute pet contest.

But, it was our cross-country adventures that initially led me to write this book. However, my decision was to write it in Byron's voice, giving this story a unique sensitivity. It is this perspective of our life together - his eyes looking back at mine -

which resulted in giving Byron many human qualities.

About a year before Byron's death, I started to keep a detailed journal about his eyes looking back at mine knowing one day I was going to be without him. That journal helped me complete the writing of this book and finalize the stories within it.

As you enjoy this book, you decide if there are times the words read like two people sharing life and love together, and whether you can decipher the line between who is the human and who is the feline.

You may laugh, cry and wonder... as well as wander across the United States on my numerous treks with Byron. You will also share those moments of tough decisions and celebrate his life.

*May you enjoy **Adventure's with Byron** as much as I enjoyed writing about my enchanting feline companion.*

Rosemary Augustine, Author

In Byron's Own Words

Born on a cold snowy night in February, 1985, I was quickly released to the outdoors and left to fend for myself. For months, I wandered the southwest side of Denver until one day I was picked up, tagged, and caged. Voices indicated I had only a few days left to live.

Then, 24 hours before D-Day (the day I was scheduled to die), a lady came in to the shelter wearing glasses and a bright blue hat. She kept tapping on the glass and making funny faces at me. She spoke to me in soft tones like music to my ears. I thought she was kind of fun, and so I stretched up on my hind legs to catch her fingers in the clutches of my paws. As I spoke to her, our spirits met, we touched, and the rest is history. Little did I know what was in store - for either of us.

My adventures started immediately. We lived in a three-story townhouse, often had parties, and had many friends over on a regular basis. I frequently explored the grounds of the townhouse complex and enjoyed sitting on the fence at night watching the night creatures.

Our cross-country treks really got me excited. We set out on many adventures in the car. An adventure is described by Webster as "an undertaking involving danger and unknown risks." OOOOOOh! I like danger and risks! The definition continues… "The encountering of risks" and last but not at all least… "A remarkable experience."

My life turned out to certainly be a remarkable experience - an adventure of a lifetime. Little did I know my life would be so full and so much fun and, provide an enchanting muse for my human partner … and eventually this book.

Let the Adventures Begin

Byron will often refer to the author - his human - as his companion or partner.

Sometimes you may not be sure who is doing the talking. Italics will differentiate between human and feline words.

When in doubt, the author suggests you just go with it, because it's probably Byron doing the speaking.

Love at First Sight

The first time our eyes met, I knew instantly I wanted to spend my life with you. Oh, how easily I was able to convince you that I was the one for you.

We embraced and touched each other's soul deeply, later learning neither of us would never be the same again.

It was a cold November night that you brought me to my new home. My heart was warmed by your mere presence. My love for you started a lifetime of joy.

My New Home

When I arrived at my new home, I was taken by the size. It was big and encompassed three floors. Two long staircases that gave me a chance to chase my imaginary friends plus there was a little garden patio with a short, stubby evergreen bush. It was probably as tall as me. I would go and explore each day and quickly assess what trouble I could get into. So far I had been able to take care of myself, so that day felt no different.

As I wandered down the driveway, there before me was an evergreen tree to match no other I'd ever seen. Taller than the buildings, this tree was my chance to see the world from the highest perch. My claws dug deep into the bark as I shimmied up through the branches. Much to my surprise, I could see only the roof of the building next to me. What happened? I'd been short changed. Not far from me was the busy roadway, with cars driving by at high speeds. It was frightening. I started to scream as loud as I could so someone would rescue me. My partner heard the racket and ran to my rescue. She was unable to reach for me, or convince me to jump into her arms for what seemed like a daring feat for an adventurous kitty. So, she sought alternative means.

As I continued to scream, bringing out the entire neighborhood - thinking I was being murdered - in drives a shiny red truck, screaming louder than me, drowning out my sounds. Before I knew it, this burley looking guy with a funny hat climbed up a ladder taller than the tree and reached for me, bringing me to safety into my partner's arms.

Would this be the last of my adventures? This was only the beginning.

My First Christmas

Not long after the episode with what I later learned was a fireman, (even though there was no fire), there was the beginning of an annual tradition with an evergreen tree inside the house. What a nice gift for me to enjoy. And how thoughtful of my partner, who must have felt sorry for me that I needed to go outside to climb a tree.

This inside tree, however, was about 8 feet tall, as it looked like it brushed the ceiling. My partner was very clever as she brought in the tree and secured it both in a pan with water (ah… how refreshing for me to drink from late at night) and with sturdy rope tied to the wall, just in case it would tip over while I was on it. Once she was done securing it, she turned to leave the room and I quickly jumped at the chance to check out my new toy.

I first checked out the pan of water that the tree trunk sat in. Hmmmm, tasty sweet water. Sniffing the branches, I could tell the sap was still fresh. But it was here that I saw my chance, looking straight up the middle of the tree trunk, and up I went. The higher I climbed the more the tree began to sway despite being tied to the wall. I didn't quiver, for I knew one day the opportunity to climb high again was in my cards when that fireman snatched me to safety.

Then suddenly, here comes my partner with boxes - lots of boxes. I wondered what could be in those boxes? I softly let out a sound not to scare her but to let her know how pleased I was with her new gift for me. But I was quickly rescued again and told just because we have a tree inside, it's not for climbing… it's only to look at and enjoy with all our treasures we will hang from it.

My first lesson in understanding the season - the Christmas season. With each year a tree, ornaments, presents, ribbon, and colorful paper adorned our living room. Often people visited and gave more presents with ribbon and colorful paper. I would get gifts as well as give them. This Christmas was the first of many to come.

The house smelled luscious with fragrances of cinnamon and cloves. The fireplace hearth and mantle were decorated too. And oh, by the way, outside the window all the green grass was now covered with some kind of cold, wet, white stuff they call "snow." Soon, in a couple of nights, we will go for a ride to see beautiful decorations outside of other people's homes. The annual tradition begins!

Years passed and each year we celebrated our annual tradition. Oh, how I enjoyed decorating the Christmas tree with you. You tastefully place each ornament as if unwrapping an individual gift.

I so enjoyed the glow of the lights, the colorful ribbon, and all the wrappings, then sitting by the tree and just enjoying its beauty and its warmth.

Every year it was a month or more of glee. Yet after all those years, living with you was like having Christmas every day.

A Lifetime of Joy

You are my pillar of strength. I watch you smile each day, even at times when you find it most difficult. When our eyes meet, it is a strengthening of each other's soul… deep to the core. You always make me smile, regardless.

I kiss your tears in moments of pain and wallow in your laughter at those moments called joy. And when we have a moment of silence, or a loss for words, I breathe deep and follow your step knowing right now, life with you is grand.

It always was and always will be the grandest of grand. What more could anyone ask for but a lifetime with you.

Dancing with You

I often dream of dancing with you
Holding you close
Stepping softly to sweet sounding serenades.

I often dream of dancing with you
On the veranda
At sunset
Soaking in the warm summer's eve.

I often dream of dancing with you
Even on cold snowy days
Because I know holding you close
Is the best way to be one with your spirit.

I look into your eyes, my kindred one,
And hold for a moment my breath
A heartbeat
And sing my song of love loudly
As I dream of dancing with you again
tonight.

Hold me close
Never let me go
And as I drift into a higher place
May the thought of dancing together linger
Beyond the dawn.

While You Were Gone

During the days and months that followed my coming to live in my new home, my partner would leave for days at a time, leaving me in the care of others who would check on me. I never liked it when she would leave, because I didn't know if she was mad at me, or if she would ever return.

Can I go with you next time my love? Why must I stay home alone? Am I really guarding the family jewels or just being safe and bored? Sometimes you say it's business, other times I know you are off on your own adventure - having fun without me. I'm not jealous, I just want to be with you.

I wait for you to return from one of your business trips. I jump each time I hear a car door slam, thinking it might be yours. I am lonely while you are gone. I count the minutes and hours that soon become days. Although neighbors feel sorry for me and share their meals or visit me, it still is not the same as having you here.

Then, I hear the key unlock the door and my heart skips a beat. I know now that I will see your beautiful face once again and feel your arms around me, whispering how much you missed me. Our time apart may have been short, but while you were gone, each day felt like a lifetime. I revel in the sweet smell of your hair and once again, have a chance to dance with you.

The Tornado

First the rain came, then the thunder and lightning. But when the siren blared out, it was time to take cover. We headed to the basement and hovered under the stairs like war-torn refugees. I trembled in my partner's arms fearing I would be taken for some unknown reason.

The windows rattled like a child desperately trying to exit a locked door. Frightened, we sat and waited for it to pass. What was minutes seemed like hours, our hearts beating to the rhythm of the torrential rain pounding against the concrete.

This was like no other storm. We had taken shelter in the past, but nothing came as close as this one. We waited - our hearts beating faster and faster. Was this ever going to end?

Suddenly, there was calm, the siren stopped,

and we emerged unscathed once again. My partner, my hero, kept me safe during one of Denver's most destructive tornados. It was May 1987, and the path missed us by only a few blocks. But the sound, oh that sound - like a freight train headed right for us. I'll never forget that sound.

This was one adventure I could have done without.

The Chicken Story

Do you remember how you always cooked chicken on the weekends? And you would sit at the dining room table and eat your feast cooked for humans?

I was bold one day and remember knocking the chicken right off your fork as you went for a mouthful. "Hey!" you said, and I said "Hey!" back. I wanted that chicken.

You went for a second mouthful and this time when I knocked it out of your hand, I hit your face in the process. Oopps! Sorry, my lovely, it's just that you're in my way of eating my favorite white meat.

I reminisce about the times I wandered the streets of Southwest Denver, and I would get plenty of chicken that was thrown in the dumpster. That chicken wasn't always tasty.

But tonight I had a plan. You didn't like me knocking the chicken off your fork, and I apologize. But, I'll get that chicken yet.

You finished your dinner and cleaned up the dishes. I watched as you carefully wrapped the remaining chicken and placed it into the fridge. You didn't realize I was watching you, even though you were talking to me the whole time. I watched you put the remaining piece of chicken that you didn't finish into the garbage. Now I just needed to wait for the right moment, hoping you will not take out the trash before bedtime.

The kitchen is clean, and we're back in the living room getting comfortable to watch a movie. It is snuggle time, but I am still working on the best time to get that piece of chicken out of the trash.

You find the right movie to watch and before we settle in, you decide to use the bathroom that is off the hall. The door is left open while you are in there.

I wait to hear when you are settled in and unable to move or jump up quickly. I saunter off the couch and quietly head to the kitchen.

I make too much noise rustling the garbage can and you call out to me. "What? I'm not doing anything" is my standard response. I then hear you say, *"Byron, you better not be in that trash... Bryon? You better not be getting that chicken out of the trash... Byron?"*

On the third call of my name, I appear at the opposite end of the hallway, looking right at you sitting in the bathroom, me with the remaining piece of chicken in my mouth dangling like a dead rat.

You are immobilized as I appear far enough away from you that there is no way you can catch me. I'm right at the foot of the stairs and can make my get away quicker than you can jump up and run after me.

I am smiling… smiling that fang grin I am so noted for because I know, "I've gottcha now." I am laughing at you, and this whole situation, because I would not be doing this had you shared your dinner with me. I am still laughing, both fangs are shining, my eyes are twinkling.

In a split second, we are both up and running… I never saw you jump so fast to chase me. Up the stairs I went to hide under the bed and eat that delicious piece of chicken - bones and all. I made sure I left no trace of what I did. You chased after me, yelling *"Don't you eat that chicken! Those bones will choke you… Bryon?"*

I have some good hiding places in our home and you never did find me or the chicken. Later that night I rejoin you on the couch to snuggle and give a silent thank you for a delicious yet forbidden piece of chicken.

Thanks for giving me a home, too. I just wanted to re-enact my days on the streets and know I was safe in the process. And, I wanted to have a little fun with you. I always love it when you start chasing after me because in human eyes I have done something unacceptable.

The best part of all this? You fed me ice cream before we finished the movie.

Cooking In the Kitchen

I'll always remember sitting with you in the kitchen while you cooked. It was a pleasure sharing that chore with you. Remember the time you filled the dishwasher and pushed "start" and then returned to cooking on the stove? You often did this.

But this time, to my surprise, within minutes, we were being engulfed in soapsuds. But your back was to me so you paid no notice.

As I called to you, you ignored my cries, thinking that I probably wanted to taste the savory dish you were cooking and your thoughts were that I had had enough.

Then, I let out a loud yell and startled you enough this time to turn and look at me, engulfed in soapsuds spewing from the dishwasher. "Turn that thing off," I thought, "and get me out of here." You quickly snatched me up and flipped the dishwasher lever to "off" … saving me once again.

As we ran from the kitchen laughing so hard that we suddenly fell down still laughing hysterically.

Dinner was not lost, but what a job cleaning up all those bubbles that climbed three feet high in the kitchen. We had a good laugh about it even years later. It is just another day of memories I'll keep with me, filled with your laughter.

More Than Just a Ride

Once again, it's more than just a ride, you drive with me by your side. I marvel as you take the helm of our 4-wheeled vessel and not once do you doubt the direction.

I smile as the sun shines upon me as we speed past cornfields, horse farms, and herds of cattle. I wave at truckers and tantalize little kids who look at me as if viewing candy in a drug store window. Such wonderment!

But whatever our destination, I am there with you supporting you along the way, comforting you in your loneliness, easing any sorrow you may have. You are my best friend. I keep your secrets deep inside me. And as we travel across this great expanse, I know we will share even more secrets, laughs and tears before we reach our final destination.

^..^
=°=

Traveling to the Unknown

You always make such good decisions for us. Never once do I quiver at the thought of our next adventure. And, once again, your caper takes us miles in a direction you choose.

I love you for your flightiness. Always on a wing, soaring high… seeing where the wind will take us next.

Getting Ready

For weeks we have gone for short rides in the car. And now, for the last two days, there seems to be chaos about with packing and scurrying to get laundry done. I know WE are going - somewhere. I just don't have a clue where or how long it will take.

It is a Thursday morning. Everything we are taking is in the car except me. I sat at my perch at the top of the stairs watching the last of the suitcases being put into the car.

My partner calls out that she is going for a walk. She left her purse at the foot of the stairs, so I know she isn't going anywhere without me and the purse. So I went and curled up on my favorite wicker chair in the spare bedroom and started to dream. The sunlight was beaming through the window.

Within 30 minutes she was back. Up the stairs she came calling for me. She woke me and started talking about us leaving. She had a bag of my toys, my brush and cans of tuna packed in my OWN overnight bag.

She told me we are going on a long adventure, that we are going to see cousin Fluffy, and that we will drive for 5 days.

She spelled out the rules of the road: *"I drive and you stay in the carrier - or else you get to drive."* Well we all know the feline's ability to drive an automobile. She kept saying, *"It's going to be an adventure Byron, and when we're done, we're going to write about our adventure."*

All I cared about was how I would miss the squirrels each morning as they ran up to the patio door, hearing the blue jays screeching outside the window, and lying in the warm sunshine each afternoon.

But, I have to go because my partner and I are going to have an adventure. Let's just see this time what this "adventure" is going to be about.

Our Cross County Trek

Day 1

I guess the real trip is happening now! We departed at 9:45 a.m. However, we ran a few last minute errands, you know - the bank and gas - the usual things when you go for an adventure. The car is packed to the gills. I am in my large carrier with a nice warm rug, a scratching pad and a "no catnip left" in a stuffed mouse.

Of course, I have a metal bowl of water, just in case I get thirsty along the way. Did my partner really think I am going to drink while she drives this car into the abyss of eastern Colorado? Instead, I knock it over within 30 minutes and get water all over the rug and my paws. She didn't put much water in the bowl to begin with, so each time she fills my water dish, I knock it over shortly thereafter.

My partner finally gets smart and puts the metal dish inside a big stone crock. No way am I going to overturn that heavy thing now, as it will crush my tender little paws.

Within an hour of riding, we stop and my partner goes for a 15 minute walk. I am fascinated with everything going on at the rest stop. You see, my carrier is sitting on the back seat with my carrier window on the side. I can see out of the back passenger window. The carrier entrance has a big gated piece that I can see out through the windshield and see her driving, reading maps (when she is lost), eating trail mix and drinking soda.

For once I am just content to sit and watch the world go by, especially when we stop at rest areas (which turned out to be a lot over the next five days). I never let out a sound while at the rest area, only when the car was moving.

Can you believe after a few hours, I am already homesick? I cry uncontrollably at times while my partner drives 75 mph across Interstate 70. She keeps saying, *"Don't cry Bryon, we're having an adventure."*

I don't want to experience this adventure! I am use to romping in 1800 sq. ft.

Then suddenly, I stop crying and look out the window and verbalize to the world passing by us, "I'm having an adventure and it's going to be fun, but it isn't fun yet! And we're going to write about this adventure" … then asking "Would you like to read about me and my adventure?" Of course, no one answers.

I keep at this for three more days. All I have to do for this adventure is go along for the ride.

So we keep driving and stopping every hour. My partner has to use the potty and of course walk. She's a fanatic about walking, but if this is going to help her drive across the country (whatever that meant), then by all means stop and walk for 15 minutes every hour. It's just going to take us six years to get wherever we are going!

When we arrive in Goodland, Kansas, my partner gets the brainy idea to take me on a leash, under a bush. I guess she thought I had to pee, but the wind was blowing soooo hard, all I wanted to do was get back into my carrier. Fortunately, it was daylight.

Had it been night time, I would have been scared to death with that wind.

So we continue to drive. As late afternoon comes, the shadows get tall and the sunlight is glistening through the windows broken by the trees as we pass them. Sun glitters dance on the inside walls of my carrier and I start to play with the shadows. I suddenly catch myself relaxing. It makes me realize I can lie down and be comfortable and catch the sun's rays as it dances on the inside of the carrier. I was being entertained and I liked it. I was stretching and playing and just plain having fun. My partner caught me "catching some rays!" My attention was diverted. It was delightful!

But as darkness fell, it started to get scary. I could no longer see out of the window because it was pitch dark. Occasionally, I would see lights, but not often. "Where are we?" I would bellow. "I guess this is Kansas." My partner called out, *"we have another 75 miles to go to reach today's destination, can you hang in there for another 75 miles?"* I cried out, "Go for it!"

By now I had to poop. How was I going to let her know? I am use to going to my litter box when the urge strikes me. And my whining and crying hasn't helped any because I have done it all day, so by now she's ignoring me. But soon she gets the message and we pull off at a Stuckey's, somewhere in Kansas.

She set up my litter box on the front seat. It was dark and lonesome behind that Stuckey's, but nobody could see the car. It took about 10 seconds to determine nobody would see me in the front seat trying to take a poop, but I had to make sure. We kitties sure like our privacy, but when you gotta go… you gotta go.

We finally make our first day's destination - Salina, Kansas. We had only travelled 347 miles in 8-1/2 hours! Don't forget, we had all those pit stops and walks! We got a room at some strange motel and spent the night. What a dump! But two important factors: they took kitties and the price was reasonable.

We got settled into the room and I was fed - finally. My partner wouldn't let me out of her sight. I was glad because I am just plain scared in a strange town and a strange motel room that smells musty. And with her being scared of the dark, we are somehow in the darkest spot of Salina. It is an end room with big evergreen bushes outside the door on a dark and lonely side street. She's not afraid of much except the dark, but tonight she was really scared. We slept with a loaded .22 revolver on the bed and huddled next to each other all night. It was comforting to know that she was more scared than me. I had to be brave for both of us - for once.

So that's the end of Day One's adventure. Boy! That's enough excitement for me for more than one day.

Day 2

The next morning after breakfast, we quickly head out for another day of driving. Next stop St. Louis! Oh boy…another day of whining, crying, and being ignored. At one point, my partner says, *"Stop crying or you can drive!"* That quickly shut me up.

Today we see lots of people at the rest stops. I actually had someone try to steal me. They couldn't open the car door so they tried to grab me through the open window. I start to hiss and growl just in time for my partner to arrive and call out, *"Hey, watch out! He'll bite you."* As the young fellow pulls his hands away from the car, he said, "Err, pretty cat." *"Yup"* she replied, *"and boy does it hurt when his fangs sink into your flesh and he draws blood."* He quickly turns away, and I cry a sigh of relief as she calls to me asking if I was OK. Is fright part of an adventure? Jeepers!

As the afternoon quickly moves into early evening, it becomes dark and time for us to stop again for the night. Oh, I can't wait to see what kind of motel we stay in tonight. We found our way to another dump, off the beaten track, and down some dark road - again. Well, all the roads are dark now… it's nighttime.

Once we settled into another kitty-friendly place, my partner decides to order pizza. What a great idea I thought. We get comfortable, she in the chair and me on the bed. Then we hear a knock on the door. She takes one look at me and I look at her and then we both look at the loaded revolver lying next to her wallet. Needless to say, the pizza delivery guy never waited for a tip.

Day 3

Day 3 was pretty much a repeat of Days 1 and 2. I continue to whine and cry and then suddenly I'd stop and stare out the window watching life go by at 75 mph.

Where are we going? Is this what humans call an adventure - driving for days to get to some unknown destination? And, are we ever going back to our home? I miss the birds and squirrels. I wonder if they are wondering what happened to me.

The hours began to blur into one another, and as the day comes to an end, I learn there is no motel that will take me. My partner says, *"Don't worry Byron, I'll find us a place to stay. I'm NOT leaving you in the car all night."*

We end up in Chattanooga, TN. The best motel we can find in Chattanooga was clean and up a flight of stairs. But it is a "No Pets" motel. Don't they realize I'm not a pet but a companion?

I snuck into a room up a long flight of stairs

and stayed hovered under the bed covers the entire time I was in the room. After my human checked in at the front desk, no one could see me being carried up the stairs under her jacket even though my big bushy tail hung out. I know I was invisible.

We are at the Chattanooga Shhhh Shhhhh Motel
Shhhhhh! Hide me!
Don't tell anyone I'm here
Sneak me in and I'll hide under the covers
I'll guard the room
Just sneak me in.

Please, put out the "do not disturb" sign
'Cause I don't want to answer the door
while you're out.

Surprise! I'm here in Chattanooga!
No, I'm not on a Cho Cho train.
I'm headed to Florida for the winter
Where it's warm and sunny.

But we had to stop in Chattanooga overnight
Where I had to hide and pretend to be
invisible … and I was!

Day 4

Well, we're almost there… almost. Another day of driving along the endless highway before us. By now I am quiet. Really, I've lost my voice, so even if I did try to say something, nothing would come out. Suddenly I'm a mute kitty. Well, you know I'm cute, but a mute? I bet my companion wishes she had a mute button days earlier.

We travel along the endless roads of Georgia, where we see peach trees, peanut farms, and cotton. But I wasn't interested in what is passing us by outside the window. I am sulking, because I miss my home. I miss taunting the birds. Will I ever see one again?

My companion is concerned, because for the first time in days I am silent. So she starts babbling, talking to me and telling me stories. When she asks me to say something *"so I know you're alive back there,"* my mouth would open, but only silence emits. Occasionally, she looks back at me or adjusts the rear-view mirror to see me. I catch her smiling. She is happy that I am silent. *"You're gonna love it when we arrive Byron, and you'll be talking up a storm, so you save that voice of yours for now."*

As we speed along the highway, I look out at the trucks passing us. If I want to scream I can't. If I'm in pain, how will she know? This is not fun and I have no way of saying so.

We spend the night in a really nice hotel. It even has an elevator. Once in the room, I head for the window sill in search of wildlife. I need to see something wild as my life certainly is not wild today. Boredom has set in. How many more days of this endless driving do I have to endure? Some adventure.

Day 5

It's a sunny morning and we head out early with excitement and enthusiasm. Not many stops today, just more driving at a speed that makes me dizzy. Something tells me I won't be riding for much longer. We don't even stop for lunch. My companion was on a mission.

"We've arrived!" Or at least that's what my partner kept yelling. *"We're here Byron, we made it. We traveled 2,000 miles, just so you can meet cousin Fluffy. Aren't you excited?"* Oh terribly! I'm jumping out of my fur! Can't you see in the rear view mirror my fur dancing in this carrier? What a sight!

My partner knows exactly where she is going. She pulls right into a driveway, and since no one is home, she knows exactly where to get the house key. She unloads some belongings including mine, and just as we are ready to take me in for the grand "Ta Da" entrance with Fluffy, Aunt Patti pulls up. She was so excited to see us, kissing and hugging us with the ultimate "squeeze to death" grip saying *"it's so good to see you I could just squeeze you to death."*

Well, anyway, we're here, in sunny southwestern Florida for the next few months. Oh boy! Is this going to be the adventure? Or now that we're off the road is the adventure over? Who knows and who cares. At any rate, I'm about to meet cousin Fluffy!

Meeting Cousin Fluffy

The first thing I noticed when I met Fluffy was his eyes - they were sad looking. He doesn't give you the impression that he's a very happy cat. After being around him for a month, I can understand why. He doesn't get much love and attention, well, not nearly as much love and attention that I get. And I think I get too much? Well I won't think that any more. I'll take all that mushiness.

Fluffy has a rather small frame for a kitty but is grossly overweight. Ha! I think everyone is overweight when you consider me and the 18 pound svelte fur ball that I am. Fluffy is a round ball of grey fluff with somewhat thinning hair. And, as a result of laying in the Florida sunshine, a good portion of him has turned blond.

Fluffy appears to be insecure about himself. He seems to be a loner and does not want, seek or get a lot of attention. So, with that, he was very guarded when meeting me. Of course, I have to be the bully and hiss at him. But Fluffy was cool, very cool. Never, in the next 3 months did he hiss at me. Not even when we were nose to nose, my fur standing straight up or me hissing at the top of my lungs, not once did he flutter. He truly had self control. He knew what it meant to be in control even if it only meant cat language.

However, his little sister Cleo, well, she doesn't walk all over him. They are affectionate to each other. There is a love affair between those two, because Fluffy's eyes definitely brighten when Cleo is around. Cleo paid no attention to me.

Fluffy would look at me inquisitively, observing my freedom, my love, my happiness. But it only made him appear sadder. Fluffy is just a few years older than me, but he doesn't jump on the counter, the table or on top of the fridge like I do. He's not too inquisitive for a feline. He mostly lies around and sleeps. And, looks for moments of love he can steal away from whoever is dishing it out that day.

He turned out to be a good buddy, despite my silliness.

After the initial stage of me barging in and taking over part of his territory, my hissing stopped and we are pleasant to each other. We'd sun together out on the porch or stalk the lizards and leave them for one another to bat around till they died. We could be in the same room together (even sitting next to each other) waiting to be fed.

Surprisingly, we are pleasant for the duration. But Fluffy knew, if he bullied me back, I'd railroad him, because I was twice his size.

Oh Fluffy, you run like someone's chasing you. You learned to relax during my presence. Fluffy, have you kept it up? I heard you developed diabetes since I left. Don't let the stresses of life get you down bud. Chill out and relax.

Fluffy, a lot has been asked of you. But you handled it - even with a bit of stress. Too much excitement, I know, makes you freak out. But hey little kitty chill out because you have a really good life now. Snoozing and cruzing on a screened-in patio the size of a house, all day long in that Florida sunshine. What a life! Life is truly a beach, a Florida beach!

A Day at the Beach

Beach? Did I say life is a Beach? Well, I finally get to see what a beach really is. It's sand! Can you believe that? Everybody talks about the beach like it's some Gift of the Gods. And all it is, is a bunch of sand!

Well, then there's water (my companion calls it an ocean) and birds. Finally I get to see some big ass birds. Jeepers, they could swoop down and carry me off they are that big. My companion calls them sea gulls. Well, I can see them alright... and I gulp at the thought of their abilities. I'll just stay close in my companion's arms for this beach visit.

The wind is strong and the air smells very

clean and fresh. I'm liking this "beach."
Well, then again, as I explore along the
sand, I get sand in my paws, yuck! And I
sink down. What is this? I fear I could be
swallowed up. And once I'm swallowed up
by the sand, then a big ocean wave will just
wash over me and I'll never be seen again.
I'm drowning just at the thought.

Over the next few months, I spend a lot of
time at the beach… Chasing seagulls and
working hard not to get my paws wet when
the water washes up on shore. The sun and
the air are relaxing for me. This is what
humans call a vacation.

Heading Home

After several months in Florida, we are heading home. Finally! I bid farewell to Fluffy and Cleo and offer the standard approval and thank you to the humans who were so kind to provide us a home these last few months. Aunt Patti and Uncle Bob were gems in their share of love for all us felines during my visit.

For the next 4 days, the ride was uneventful. The excitement of an adventure had worn off and I was anxious to get home and see my friends. I salivated at just the thought. The warm climate during the winter months made me lazy. I wasn't use to 80 degrees in January. I'm anxious to see snow, feel the cold and stalk the birds as they feed outside the windows.

But the trip through Texas leaves me pondering life. We get lost going through Dallas, looking to exit off the highway to buy gas. Once we find an exit with a gas station and convenience store there is a sigh of relief.

While my companion is pumping gas, I can see into the truck in front of us. Shotguns are proudly displayed across the back window. I started to shake. Then I look over at the clerk in the window of the convenience store and he's holding a shotgun. I'm silent, but shaking in fear of my life. And then I think to myself, "Wait a minute, I'm just a cat, they aren't interested in me."

My companion quickly gets back into the car and we drive off hoping any bullets miss us. My companion blurts out, *"Whew, that was a close call, eh Byron?"* She looks into the rear view mirror to make sure we are not being followed. And I thought Colorado was the wild west!

Once home, it is so good to be back stalking the squirrels outside the window. And it feels good to chase my imaginary friends up and down the stairs.

The Cat Spa

My companion is scurrying frantically these past few days. But this morning while sitting on the sink as she showered, I notice my travel bag that was filled with all my stuff on the last adventure is now filled with all her stuff. As I paw through it, I notice soap, deodorant, toothpaste and Listerine. Yuck! I use none of these.

Puzzled, I head down the steps and at the bottom of the stairs is a huge tote bag with some of my canned food, my toys and the red polar fleece jacket that I love to curl up in. Suddenly I know, we are both going on an adventure, but this time separately.

I don't want to be alone on my adventure. My companion and I always have fun when we go somewhere, why can't I go with her this time? Well, my partner later notices my pouting and sits me on her lap for a talk.

She explains that this time I am going to have my own adventure. A new experience staying at the "Cat Spa." She says, *"Byron,*

I am traveling to a place where I can't take you, I hope you understand. You will have lots of attention and plenty of your own things at the Cat Spa." She says, *"You adjusted so well at cousin Fluffy's, this will be a piece of cake."* I'm thinking I adjusted so well because you were there with me. But this time I'll have to put my mind to it and like it, because at this point, there is no choice, the decision is made.

The car is loaded with my belongings and off we drive to Wheat Ridge, Colorado to the Cat Spa. Once there I realize we have been there just a few days before checking it out. The surroundings are familiar, the faces friendly. We are greeted warmly, the gals are just gushing over me.

We are escorted to my "kitty condo," a private two story suite with its own outdoor playroom. My unit is multi-story with both indoor and secure outdoor sections, so I get to see lots of wildlife, have the sun shine on me daily. Best of all, I have my favorite rug, toys and the red fleece jacket I so love to curl up in. I'll miss my companion while she's off on her adventure.

The Cat Spa - Wheat Ridge, CO

As the weeks go by I am King! I receive lots of attention. And, I ruled the cat house as the other kitties were more than accommodating to let me be the boss. Not once did I hiss. This was home. Well, it was the next best thing to a home away from home.

During the day, we were all on our best behavior and played with our care takers. At night, all us cool cats sat up talking our cat talk, telling high tales and scary stories. We were located in a wooded area, so the night shadows were frightening. As I sat on my perch, I howled at the moon and slept comfortably night after night.

Then the party was over. What seemed like just a few days was several weeks and my companion arrives back from her adventures to claim me and take me home. Bye bye my cool cats. Keep howling at the moon and write when you get work.

$$^..^$$
$$=^o=$$

Over the next six months, Byron stayed at the Cat Spa three separate times for a total of 11 weeks. He was their favorite guest.

A New Kid Comes to Live with Us

It is about 6 a.m. and there is a knock on the front door. Who is waking me up? It's our neighbor Annie, with a little furry something in her hand. I couldn't quite make it out. Their conversation is quiet, not for me to hear. Hmmmm, I wonder what's going on?

I step closer to the front door. Suddenly my partner is in full care-taking mode with a box, towel, a bowl of milk and some of my food. What? My Food?

I can barely see through the screen door to see what she is doing on the porch, but she is doing something and I want to know.

Then I hear an all too familiar sound and I started to hiss. Another cat coming into my territory? No Way!

This is no ordinary cat. It is a badly injured 4 week old kitten that looks like it has been beat up with cuts all over its face and body. Possibly the thorny bushes got it. Story has it that it was left for dead in the bushes behind our building.

It whimpered and cried and made a weak meow sound. And I hissed and growled to show my disapproval of my partner's lovingness to another.

She spends the next 2 hours on the porch with this half dead kitten while I am on the other side of the screen, voicing my disapproval.

The next thing I know, she picks up the kitten and gets into the car and drives off. Where in the hell is she going with a half dead kitten at 8 o'clock in the morning?

A few hours later, they return, much to my dismay. While my partner gives me a good talking to about what is going on, she begins to corner off parts of the kitchen and bathroom. Suddenly, I am going to share - my life, my home, my partner with this kitten. I'm steaming!

You see, I learn later that my partner was asked to take the kitten to the animal shelter to be put up for adoption. But when she got to the shelter's parking lot she realized the kitten was so sick (hours from death), he would have been put to sleep that same day.

Still in the car, she began to cry as she felt a warm sensation on her thighs. Not only did that kitten pee on her, it crawled up her chest and licked her tears as she sobbed about the fate of this injured animal.

I believed her story, as she is a sucker for affection and this kitten won her heart. Instead of dropping him at the pound, she drove straight to the vet and asked for help.

Doc Reinhart is more than helpful when he learned of this kitten's fate. He examined it, gave my partner some medicine at no charge and gave pointers to bringing it home to me with the idea of nursing it back to health - and eventually finding it a home.

All I can think of is how much attention is going to be taken away from me. I have lots of attention now… how can that possibly continue with this little runt intruding on my territory. Needless to say, I am not happy.

Days turn into weeks and this little kitten steals the show. Lavished with affection, he just doesn't seem right to me. He is also fascinated by my whiskers and would constantly touch my face. Eventually it appears that the exercise of finding this kitten a good home is already done. This is going to be his permanent home. As for me? Well, I now have a new play toy!

As this little guy grows, so does my annoyance. He is named Maxx. And he keeps running into walls and doorways and always wants to cuddle up to me. I am not his mother, but he sure thinks I am.

Months after joining our home, I learn that Maxx is blind. Blinded at birth - which now makes sense why he was left for dead in the bushes. He was also diagnosed with some malady in his brain that the Doc only gave him 2 years to live.

That little ball of fur turned out to be the best thing for me as it added years to my life. I would chase him up and down the steps constantly, so I got some very good exercise.

We had our ups and downs, since I would often try to choke him (he annoyed me so much). But in the end, he turned out to be a loving and supportive friend that outlived me.

We spent the next 11 years together and although he had his quirks, he turned out to be my best buddy.

....

The Big Green Monster

From the very first day that Max arrived on the scene, it is noticeable he is different. Especially different from me. Always looking over his shoulder, like someone was coming after him.

I couldn't quite figure it out at first. But as time went on, it became real apparent to me that Maxx was suffering from Green Monster Syndrome! The Big Green Monster was real alright.

This was no imaginary monster, like some of my playmates that I have invented over the years. This sucker was BIG, GREEN and LIVING IN OUR BASEMENT! It came out to chase us on weekends and scare us into hysteria. Maxx more so than me.

You see, I've been living with The Big Green Monster all my life and just didn't know it. Maxx makes me realize how terrifying this monster really is.

I'm not quite sure the very first time IT

happened, but it definitely took my partner and me by surprise. She was settling up and cleaning one Sunday, and decided to run the vacuum.

Now keep in mind, I've been living with her for seven years and only once did she chase me with the vacuum (it was turned off). She was in a playful mood and was chasing me saying, *"I'm gonna gettcha" I'm gonna gettcha,"* laughing the whole time. I was pretty sure she was kidding, but I had to act as if this was for real and so I ran and hid for awhile.

But this particular Sunday, was a little different. And Max went nuts. The noise was incredibly ear deafening for him. You see because Maxx is blind, so his hearing is over compensated. I ran and hid and so did Maxx.

However, when it was all over, he was in such pain he cried, howled, hissed, growled and performed every other sound a frightened animal could do. He just about attacked my partner and wanted to kill her. But thankfully he didn't.

It took him days to calm down. That's when the drugs came on the scene.

Shortly after this episode, Maxx started a program of Valium. A quarter table every other day, to take the edge off of this crazy episode.

About two weeks went by, and out came the Big Green Monster again. And again he was drugged. And, again Maxx had the same reaction despite the drugs.

As time went on, my partner vacuumed less and less. The rugs were getting in pretty bad shape and really needed to be vacuumed weekly with all our hair. Maxx was off the drugs by now and appeared OK.

Then one warm, sunny Sunday, Maxx went out on the patio. He was having a good time playing in the garden, nosing the ground cover and smelling that stubby little evergreen bush. Since he was no longer drugged, he was in heaven enjoying the fresh air and sunshine immensely.

I joined him and shortly thereafter, my partner closed the door. I had a pretty good idea of what was going to happen next.

While I watched over Maxx, she tackled that Big Green Monster. I could hear the noise faintly behind the closed door.

Maxx was scared, he knew something was going on, and that the Monster had come out, but it wasn't quite close enough. The Monster's growl was in the distance.

Nonetheless, Maxx crouched down and was ready to attack if that Monster suddenly came through the door. And, then there was silence. Had my partner conquered the Big Green Monster? She opened the door to let us know of her victory.

From then on, we experienced the Big Green Monster every Sunday afternoon. And every time, we would go out on the patio by the evergreen.

After all the noise ended, my partner would emerge victoriously announcing the Monster was conquered. *"My kitties are safe once again,"* she says to us lovingly.

Hugging each of us simultaneously, she says, *"You know I would never let any harm come to either of you. Byron knows that because he's lived here for so long. You'll know that too, one day, Maxx. You will understand that I will never let any harm come to you while you are in my home."*

And with that Maxx weeps with joy while I gloat at the fact that this is really true. It's just going to take Maxx a long time to really understand how safe we really are.

^..^
=°=

Byron Meets Drac

A friend came to live with us for a few weeks and he brought his cat with him. The cat was named Drac - short for Dracula!

Drac was solid black with piercing green eyes. We weren't sure this was going to work as Drac was #3 in the household (Maxx was #2). So Drac was situated on the patio to be safe and away from my bullying antics.

But, one day when the humans were gone, I left my warm spot on the bed and ventured out into the living room and over to the sliding screen door. I wanted to settle the score of who was in charge in my home. I didn't appreciate a third cat honing in on my territory, and especially that I could not go on the patio to enjoy the warm air with the option to catch a bird or two.

Drac was asleep on the patio chair - my chair. I quietly dug my claws into the screen and slid the screen door open. Drac opened one eye. He didn't cower. I entered his temporary domain and walked right up to him. He now had both eyes wide open staring at me in fear. He jumped down to be faced to face with me. No words were spoken only the ice stare I gave my prey.

Drac wasn't sure what was next, but I knew. I came to let him know who is boss. I wacked him good across the nose drawing blood. Shoke with disbelief, Drac returned to his spot on the chair and I returned to my warm bed. We never came face to face again. Drac stayed with us for 43 days. And to this day he never ratted on me. Smart Kitty!

Drac never ratted on Byron, however, when the humans returned home and saw the screen door ajar and blood on Drac's nose, the humans could only imagine that a wild animal must have jumped up on the patio and scared him to where he tried to open the screen to safety.

Once Again We Drive Off

Once again we prepare for a cross country drive. But this time I learn it's a permanent move. All our household belongings are put into 2 big wooden containers for shipment. Where are we going this time? How long will it take? And now with Maxx, what if one of us has to poop?

Our partner made us very comfortable. We had the entire back seat of our 4-door Volvo. Two carriers joined together for our comfort across the leather seats.

This trip I didn't have much say, I knew the routine and I really didn't want to make Maxx nervous. Especially in and out of pet friendly motels. But it was an exciting six long days across this expansive country. I summarized the trip to my former vet, Doc Reinhart. He had been my veterinarian for most of my life. I was sad to leave Denver as I knew I would never see him again. Here's what I wrote him:

August 13, 2001

Hi Doc Reinhart,

Wanted to let you know that Maxx and I made the cross-country trip from Colorado to New Jersey safe and sound with our human companion.

She's a slow driver. It took us 6 days to go 1835 miles. She fixed us up in the back seat with two carriers joined together so Maxx and I could have lots of room to snuggle.

Much of the time I was busy looking out the window watching the world go by while Maxx slept. He didn't mind the ride at all. He just settled in and never a meow. A few times our companion wondered if we were even in the car – we were so quiet.

The drive was long but the weather was perfect. We rode with the windows open and had lots of fresh air. When we stopped at the Rest Areas, we had lots of attention from other people traveling – some with their kitties too. A few people even came up to the car and petted me. No one tried to steal me this time. The Rest Areas were really cool as most of the time we stopped under a shade tree so we didn't get too hot in the sun.

Of all the motels we stayed in, only one was not pet friendly. We snuck in anyway. The best part of the drive was a really neat motel in Indiana. They took kitties. Our room was on the upper floor of this motel. I was able to get up on the windowsill and look out. Just below our window a family staying at the motel had their cows grazing right off the parking lot. They were pretty big cows but they were quiet, only moo'd a few times.

It was a real friendly motel. Our companion stopped and talked to another traveler with a doggie while she was carrying me in. But I just can't get over those cows in Indiana! I remember seeing cows once before when I traveled to Florida with her years ago.

However, our companion got a little nervous

with us in the car about 75 miles from our destination. We broke down and had to pull off to the side of the road and wait for help. That was our last day of travel and it was starting to get pretty hot too.

She found a shady spot for us to park under even though she had to drive with the flashers on at about 10 mph until she found such a spot. Some nice police officer helped us after about 45 minutes along the side of a very busy 2-lane road. It was only the muffler that we lost, so we were off driving in no time.

We got settled into our new home as soon as we arrived. However, the furniture didn't come for almost 3 weeks so there wasn't much for me to scratch or sit on. Though my partner was smart, she packed my favorite scratching post. Where did she have that in the car? We were so loaded down but she managed to squeeze things in between the cracks.

Maxx slept in the closet for the first 2 weeks. But I joined my partner on the patio and at night on our make shift bed. Boy was I glad when the furniture arrived. I could finally sleep on the bed and get off the darn floor!

The best part of living in southern New Jersey is our screened patio. It overlooks trees, a grassy field and lots of flowers. The birds sing to us day and night, and there are lots of squirrels to excite me.

At night the lightning bugs startle me with their sudden flashes of light. There are a few wild kitties that chase the squirrels. And, there are also bunny rabbits. Little brown bunnies with puffy white tails. It's a good thing we're up on the 2nd floor and screened in. Of course, at my age it's better just to fantasize.

We visited our new Vet Doc – Doc Blumenthal at Animal Hospital of Millville. He's pretty neat and the entire staff fussed over us – just the way we like it. They loved Maxx - he's now 25 lbs. Doc wants me to come back in October for blood work - he thought it best after the stress of moving settles down. His waiting room was pretty cool. He had aquariums with snakes and lizards and turtles. Besides kitties and doggies, he takes care of birds and reptiles too. His office is nestled in the woods. It's really a cool place.

Well just wanted you to know we've arrived. Our companion took pictures of us while we were traveling, so I've included them. We miss Colorado but have adjusted to the humidity here in the east – except for those scorching 100 degree days when I enjoy the sunshine cause it feels so good on my old bones, and Maxx wants to sit right in front of the air conditioner to get cool. This last heat wave was pretty unusual and we hope we don't have too many of those again. We've been getting lots of rain so my partner is ready with the flea medicine.

Tell all our friends at Park Hampden - Hello. We miss you,

Love Byron and Maxx

^..^
=º=

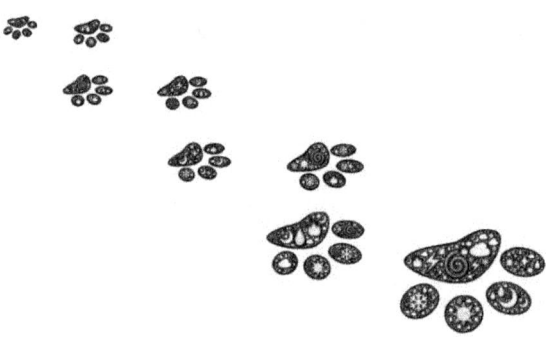

Starting to Countdown

Regular journal entries started 9 months prior to Byron's death. These entries continue to be in Byron's voice - writing about him watching me watch him. At times it would be eerie to think he would voice these words, have these thoughts. In watching him watch me, it gave me a depth to my words I would not have found otherwise.

^..^
=º=

Unconditional Love

As you stroke my hair
and touch my face fondly,
I know in your heart your love for me
is unconditional.
You never expected anything in return.

Love is grand, deep and eternal.
No bond as deep as ours
could ever be severed.
It is with deep spiritual connection
My love for you is returned
each time I kiss you tenderly.

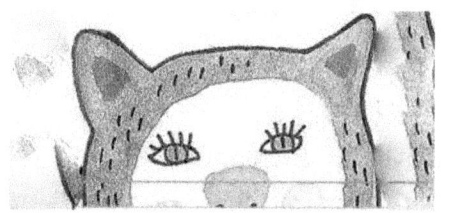

Watching You Sleep

I watch you sleep peacefully
Re-charging your being for another day.
Your daily routines are rote by now
Easily achieved
Constantly practiced.

As you lay in the sunshine
Soaking in nature's gold
Your veins are charged once again
With strength to start another day.

September 2002

My Dearest Rosemary,

Yesterday you were kind in taking me to the doctor. You can always tell when I'm having one of my bad days or when I'm just not up to snuff. The news was not promising. Though I have many months left to live, you listened to the words the doctor spieled, knowing our time would soon end.

Rejoice in our years together. Reminisce of all our fun times, trying moments and never to be forgotten side-splitting, tension-halting experiences. You were always good at that…keep the humor coming.

May I remind you that I'm not gone yet, so do not begin your grieving until long after the soil is dumped on my wooden box.

Or better yet, keep my ashes in an urn tucked neatly beside your favorite antique clock on the mantel. I'll be glad when those clocks stop chiming, knowing I'll finally be at rest and at peace.

Do not grieve for me with the burden of knowing my illness. My fate is not yet sealed. I may surprise you and defy fate living well beyond expectations. By then you will have shed enough tears to fill a river. May I suggest you look positively at our life together and treasure those moments past, present and even the future ones to come.

You made me laugh aloud so many times, like when I stole the piece of chicken and the dishwasher overflowing with soap. And, the drive cross-country to Florida with the suggestion that I drive. You were a pleasure, a joy, and a symphony of laughter that brought with it a tenderness to hold you tightly, deep into the night.

As I glance at you across the room, I peer deep into your soul to understand your thoughts and try to help you understand mine. I have a love for you so deep no words can ever express. And that love expects none in return. Yet unknowingly, you gave as much as I and even more. We make a good team, strange partners to some. My heart is one with yours. Your soul, your very presence makes me smile even on a rainy day. I wait to see your sunshine each morning, feel your touch and know you are one with me too.

Your treats are sinful. Bad for my teeth, my weight, and my overall health. But it is with these treats that my life is extended because your treats are filled with love. With so much love, one could never have too much.

As Always,
With Love…
Your Byron

Another journal entry a few months later ...

Rejoice My Love

Rejoice my love, as I hear you crying in the night, off in the distance, and in the morning in the shower. Don't cry my love, don't mourn my passing. Rejoice in all the splendor of the years we spent together. The love we created, the joy we shared, the strength we gave each other in times of gloom. You were my pillar when tornado warnings hit and we hovered in the basement like war-ravaged citizens. And those hot summer nights when lightning strikes abounded, we hid under the sheets… each protecting the other if only from fear.

Rejoice in these moments and many others. Rejoice my love because I too will miss you and those wonderful moments. Let me kiss the wet from your tears and soak the moisture into my bones to give me strength to live another day. Don't cry my love but rejoice in the splendor of our life-long relationship of loving each other.

I Feel Your Pain

I feel your pain today, and I try to comfort you. I know you are sad about things in your life. I try to comfort you, hold you, and kiss you. I do not try to move away when you hold me too tight for too long. I too need your strength. No illness or lack of focus will matter in the end.

Your Secrets Are Safe With Me

I remember our first kiss. And, the first time I told you I loved you. You were shocked... beyond belief, lightly tapping me on my cute black nose. Why? I could not understand. My kiss was only to signify the pleasure of your company. A love bite to gently seal my love for you.

I did not falter, but instead, accepted your idea of tenderness. It was cold. But within time you warmed your heart to me, sharing your deepest feelings, secrets and desires. Many kisses followed along with expressions of love shared between us.

I go to my grave knowing things about you that no one will ever know. It is my pleasure to die with your secrets tucked safely inside me never to be voiced aloud.

Coming to Terms with the End

Journal entry - early morning June 13, 2003

It's early and I feel I must come to terms with the end. It is time to put Byron to rest. With fluid around his heart and lungs and not able to get it out, it's only a matter of time. So I ask myself, "What's more humane... letting him die naturally or letting him die peacefully? Will he understand? What does he prefer?"

Listening and watching him breathe in the night I feel he's suffering. I am more than willing to do the ultra sound that the vet suggests, but I think his chances for a full recovery back to 100% are not realistic. He has slid down to below 50% in just a couple of days. He's not eating and he's on drugs. And at 18-1/2 years and having had this progressing for some time, he will not, I don't feel, fully recover. It's time.

As I write in my journal, I ask "What's the right thing to do?" Here is what I wrote:

Die at home naturally means:
Choking for his last breath, heart attack in the night, pain and suffering for him. This benefits me in keeping him alive, but does not benefit Byron, as Byron is the one suffering.

Die peacefully means:
Time it, say good-bye, and know that it's for the best, since his quality of life has diminished so much. I know he won't fully recover and that he'll only decline further. He'll die peacefully in my arms.

I knew when his quality of life diminished, where he had more bad days than good, I knew I would have to make a decision.

My love, my soul mate, his eyes tell me it's time to go. He holds on clinging to the notion – soon. It's only a matter of when.

Today Byron, you will go where there is endless sunshine, birds and squirrels, green grass and trees. You will be at peace, comfortable, healthy and live eternally in your heaven. You go knowing you are loved and cherished and that you will be greatly missed. This gives you an opportunity to pass on peacefully. Know that you will always be in my heart.

You touched my soul deeply for 18+ years and one day we will meet again in a special place. Meanwhile, I'll accept your spirit and know you are with me always. You will relish your new found place of peace and quiet, undisturbed, smiling upon those of us who are left, and giving us strength to continue on without you.

You know Byron that you are deeply loved. You will always be in my heart. It is with a deep love for you that I take you to this peaceful place. A peaceful love-filled departure is only fitting for the one I've loved for so long.

You are a part of me. So a piece of my heart goes with you. How lucky I am to have had you love me for as long as you did. Though I know you will still love me long after you are gone. You will be with me in spirit. There will be times I will feel your presence and will see you reach out for me. Never did I think you'd live this long. Thank you for 18 wonderful and loving years.

I will not cry but will remember all the love that we shared and the hearts that we touched during our 18 years together. You will always be ... enchantingly unforgettable.

^ .. ^
= o =

Just Before You Go

We facie the closing hour as we sit as a family enjoying the patio for the last time together. Maxx rubbing against the screen, me with a cup of chamomile tea and Byron sitting comfortably under my chair. He's ready for it to be over and is thankful I made the decision. Maxx will miss him as Byron has been part of Maxx's life since he was born 11 years prior.

A few more trains will pass by on the tracks. And, soon the noise will stop. It will be quiet and the sun will shine forever. I'll miss you Byron. I'll always love you.

Soon you'll be at peace.

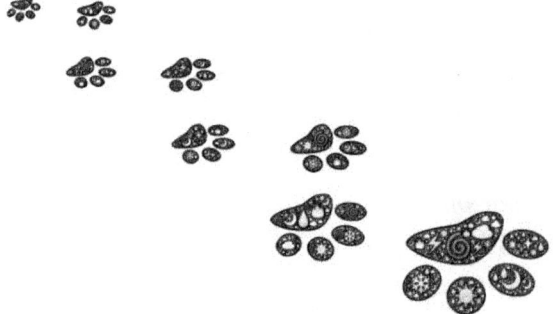

Our Last Moments

It's harder and harder to breathe
I have moments I feel great
and I'm ready to chase the wind
And then fatigue overcomes me.
I can barely eat, I just want to be still
Enjoy the moment
Know you are close
Smell your fragrance as it passes me with
the gentle wind.

I am ready for a greater place
Where sunshine and birds
grace the lawn daily
Where I have energy and can play for hours
I have told you so many times before
how much I love you
This moment is no different.

I know our paths will cross again.
Thank you for a lifetime of love,
A life of joy and peace,
A life of wonder and adventure,
A life of friendship and enchantment.
May you always feel my presence.
Know that I'm just a touch away.

And may you feel me kiss you each night
And smile at you each dawn.

Don't cry my love
It's time to say goodbye
It's time for me to go
If it's hard for you to decide
Let me tell you it's time.

My spark is not as bright
My step is slowed
And, although I know
You are there next to me
I'm still uncomfortable.

No more pills
No more needles
Just let me watch the sunrise and listen to
the birds have their morning feed.
I hear the train in the distance
And a voice that says let's go.

I resist because I do not want to leave you.
Your heart is broken before I've even left.
I know no one can ever fill my shoes
No one can ever take my place.
The bond we shared was special

That bond will not break with my departure
But only strengthen because I know
you cared enough to let me die peacefully.

As I lay here and look into your sad eyes
Good bye my love, be strong
For it is you that I look to
To carry my strength beyond time
One day we will meet again
But meanwhile you must go on

As I lay here and look up at you
I give you one last smile
To acknowledge
that everything's going to be alright
We made it this far
It's been a good life
I would not have traded one moment.

Good bye my love
Remember our good times together
How I made you laugh
How much I loved you
How I shared so much of your life
And, always remember
when you walked by me
How I would reach out for you.

It's time to go…
As you hold me in your arms
And comfort me … this is the end.
You whispered gently at my closing breath
"Anytime you want me,
just think of me and I'll be there"

Your very last words I heard were
"I love you"
And then I breathed my last breath.
You cried softly and held me gently
You stayed with me
for what seemed like hours afterwards
Holding me and stroking me

I know one day we'll be together
Let those who knew me
Know of my passing.

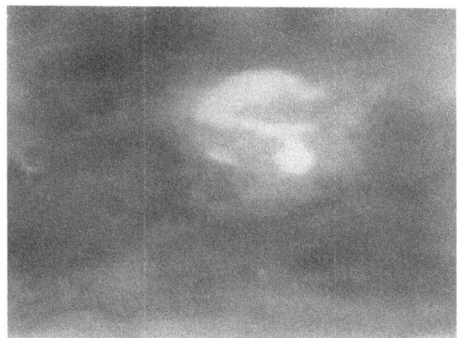

He's Gone

A final journal entry ...

The rain came shortly after you died to cry a sea of tears with me. It rained for what seemed like hours washing my hurt of your loss. You were ready. You had no fear. I was fearful that I was doing the right thing. It was right. No more pain. No more needles, no more drugs. The heavens are joyous with thunder of your arrival, lighting up the sky with streaks of lightning, raining harder, healing my pain.

Rejoice in the splendor of the rain as Byron dances with his new friends.

Soon after the rain, a little bird came up on my patio railing. I have never had birds come to the railing before this moment. I felt it was you singing me a song saying how happy you are now.

When I hear the birds now, I will think of you.

Death

*Death is so final, it comes like a thief in the
night, taking with it life, memories and love.
Stripping you to the bone
to recover, but never completely.*

*Death is so complete, it is the link that
completes the circle of life from beginning to
end, never knowing where it starts or where
it finishes, though you know in your heart
this is the end.*

*Death ... dark, fast,
uncompromisingly cunning to the quick,
it takes you down, never to get up again.*

*Death is the last goodbye,
words never to be spoken again,
words heard for the last time,
Words that are a whisper...
just a whisper
Silencing all.*

*Death is the end ...
end of the road,
end of life's journey,*

*the end of the story.
Death snuffs out life,
extinguishes the beauty we once knew
and finalizes all that once was.*

*Death of someone you love so much is final.
It creates emptiness
and deepens the void
that was filled for years.*

*I no longer have you to hold in my arms,
spend my days with,
whisper how much I love you
and worry about how I will care for you.*

Byron – In Loving Memory

February 1, 1985 – June 13, 2003

June 13, 2003

Berwyn, PA - *Byron was laid to rest today at 3:35pm in Paoli, PA where he will be cremated and his ashes will remain with his long time companion, Rosemary Augustine. Although he battled kidney failure for three years, and was very ill for the last month, it was only in the closing days the doctor discovered advanced heart disease. Excessive fluid had accumulated around the heart and lungs making it difficult for him to breathe.*

Byron had a full life. He was rescued from a shelter 18+ years ago. With his human companion, he enjoyed 7 different homes, 5 cars, 2 relocations, 4 vets, lived in 3 states and traveled cross-country twice. He loved to ride in the car until recently. He had many friends including Maxx, his buddy and brother for 11 years, Drac, Annie's dog Bear, and Zar as well as numerous birds, squirrels, rabbits, seagulls and deer. His favorite spot... laying anywhere in the sunshine. His best moment was when he appeared in the hallway with a piece of chicken dangling from his mouth like a dead rat. His best kept secret was whacking Drac! An avid fan of kitty aerobics in his early years, his first Christmas he climbed the tree!

Byron was greatly loved, and many were in awe of him. He had a presence when entering a room, and had the ability to command attention instantly. Many called him enchanting as he won your heart over and over.

He is survived by his human companion Rosemary Augustine, his buddy and brother Maxx, and numerous friends and acquaintances who will fondly remember him.

His companion Rosemary says, "Byron will now be where there is eternal sunshine, birds and trees. Although he is now in a peaceful place, he will always have a place in my heart. The love of my life for 18+ years, may he rest peacefully at an eternal oasis."

Now with Every Passing Year

With every passing anniversary, candles and memories are part of a memorial service performed each year – to remember Byron's life, his love, and his mark on the world.

"Even now, years after Byron's death, he is still very much a part of my life – if only in memory" says his companion Rosemary. "A love touched so deep, no human bond could break, and today, that love is still deep in my heart."

With writing this book, a healing process took place. A life of 18+ years passes quickly, yet memories linger well beyond 100 years or more. Byron was enchanting. A unique individual of feline nature, with a personality of human qualities.

Writing this book gave the author an opportunity to move forward with other feline companions, first with Maxx and later with Ziggy and Zack. However, most of this was written when Byron was still alive. The author's daily journal during his last year of life gave her a glimpse into how much love – unsuspecting love – was showered upon her during those 18+ years. And that love, later to be shared with humans, was a deep and lasting unconditional love never experience prior to Byron.

"I treasured my time with Byron," says the author. *"And, I treasure my experience in having such a loving companion who knew me, understood me and never wavered at whatever decision I made."*

Byron ...
In Another Time And Space...

^..^
=°=

A New Dimension

Ziggy and Zack came on the scene 10 years ago as kittens and have their own books: ***Secrets I Learned From Ordinary House Cats*** *and* ***Ziggy's Secrets****.*

Together, Ziggy and Zack were adventurous in their own right. However, Zack died suddenly at age 9 leaving Ziggy lost and grief stricken.

However, on this day, Ziggy shares with you in his own words, his meeting with Byron...

I keep seeing this figure on the computer screen. A stately statue of a beautiful tux man. Occasionally, I get called Byron and then she corrects herself. She tells me she's writing a new book about an old love. She had a lot of old loves, but this one she kept the flame burning. I guess I can see why now. She has an equal amount of fire for me though, so I guess you can have two loves in your life. You make room in your heart. There's always room for one more.

It was a special day I met Byron. But I'll let Byron tell the story because he's so good at the adventure side. I'm good at the short quips I'm so known for on Facebook (see him on Facebook at ***Ziggy's Secrets***).

However, it was an interesting day. An adventure as Byron calls it…

Bryon Meets Ziggy.

It was a warm day in July, Ziggy was home alone and sound asleep on the patio. Something about those patios, my partner always made sure we had an outdoor patio that was safe and secure.

I didn't want to startle Ziggy, I wanted to quietly just "be" with him as he slept. I was invisible now, so Ziggy would only feel my energy. He was good at sensing energy - positive or negative. My spirit would occasionally float in and out visiting my partner. And, she would always know it's me. But I wanted to meet Ziggy this time.

More than 10 years have gone by since my passing. Well, 12 to be exact. Ziggy was solo now as Zack passed 9 months prior to this entry point. Ziggy had a lot of grief and separation anxiety that prevented me from arriving sooner. He was ready now to meet me and open to the journey we would take together. And Ziggy would understand completely what was expected of him as I prepared for my arrival.

So, on that warm summer day that I knew we'd be home alone together, I appeared. Ziggy was surprised to see me "come alive" so to speak since he only ever saw pictures of me. "Well Hello" was his first words and I responded "Hello" back to him. As I explained to him our journey, I assured him we would not leave the patio, that our journey was only via our minds and that my partner (well, really our partner) knows the transfer that is about to take place. She welcomed the journey.

And so the journey began in our minds. Understanding the transfer of power - the feline power of love. Ziggy had most of it already but I was to instill the greatest power yet - the power of self-forgiveness. You see, Ziggy's anxiety interfered with his joy. He was so disappointed when his brother Zack died, that he felt a part of him died too. I was here to tell him it's not so. How our hearts can continue to love and experience joy and forgiveness in another dimension. Ziggy was aware of that dimension, but feared going there. My job was to take him and share with him the ease in which he could be in that new dimension and "our" partner would still be with us.

As we shared our stories of love, peace and joy, forgiveness was his biggest stumbling block. He felt cheated that Zack left and didn't pass on the power so he felt short changed, hurt, lost, even angry at times that he, Ziggy, couldn't fill the shoes of loving himself unconditionally. He had become very insecure. Most importantly, he couldn't accept his fate of forgiving himself - which was so important for him to overcome his separation anxiety.

I taught Ziggy how to forgive himself and in doing so, a wave of relief came over him instantly. It was a simple exercise of accepting that Zack had completed the work he came here on earth to do and that Ziggy still had much more life to share. Forgiving himself was just as important as loving himself unconditionally.

We spent the next few hours playing in a green meadow nearby, taking turns catching bugs and birds and sharing in our catches.

We shared a bond and a love for our human companion that was deep and lasting beyond time and space.

We exchanged words as only felines do with a deep understanding of what we were experiencing. Ziggy knew he was to return with a new found knowledge of love and peace. Someone to carry the torch and continue the adventures in Byron's honor.

Byron was pleased with Ziggy's openness to receive. He knew his work was completed. Bryon said he will visit from time to time so they can play in the green meadow.

Byron parted as the front door opened and a voice called out, *"Ziggy, I'm home."* Byron knew it's Ziggy's turn to now be the King Kat of the Augustine household.

As Ziggy returns to reality, he jumps for joy seeing his partner and begins to verbalize his last few hours. His partner is all ears even though she doesn't understand a word he is saying.

She knows he is happy and telling her of his dream and she imagines he is telling her how he met Byron.

For an instant she sees a flash of black fur and knows Ziggy had a welcomed visitor. Byron was up to his tricks, even in the after life. She smiles and knows it was just the beginning of a new companion for Ziggy.

"God Bless the felines that have graced my life" she says aloud, *"regardless of the time and space."*

^..^
=º=

About the Author

A native of southern New Jersey, Rosemary Augustine spent most of her adult life living in California and Colorado and returned to the Philadelphia area in 2001 to care for an aging parent.

Rosemary calls herself a Journal Aficionado (her License Plate reads: Journal)... as she is an avid writer, including a daily journaling practice. She writes fiction and non-fiction books.

Her artistic endeavors include acrylic painting and mixed media collages, and she also designs hand-crafted journals that she gives as gifts and often sells. She is the author of numerous books and is listed in Who's Who of American Women and Who's Who in the World.

Rosemary continues to write and publish books, paints and honors her creative spirit.

In 2015, she relocated to Melbourne, FL with her famous cat "Ziggy" - who has his own Facebook page: *Ziggy's Secrets*, and his own website:
www.ThankGodImaFeline.com

Books by Rosemary Augustine:
Adventures with Bryon
Secrets I Learned From Ordinary House Cats
Ziggy's Secrets
365 Days of Creative Writing
Journal to a More Creative Self
Bucket List Journal
29 Things To Do
I Love My Job
How To Live and Work Your Passion
Facing Changes In Employment

Visit the author online at:
www.RosemaryAugustine.com

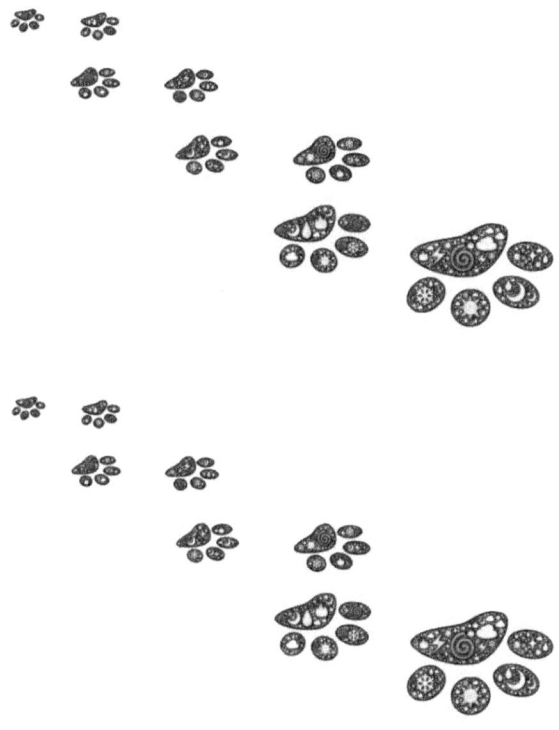

Byron Lives On . . .

```
 ^ . . ^
= ° =
```

www.ingramcontent.com/pod-product-compliance
Lightning Source LLC
Chambersburg PA
CBHW071724090426
42738CB00009B/1874